One day at a time

Healthy habits tracker

Month ___________

Year ___________

Days

1												
2												
3												
4												
5												
6												
7												
8												
9												
10												
11												
12												
13												
14												
15												
16												
17												
18												
19												
20												
21												
22												
23												
24												
25												
26												
27												
28												
29												
30												

Healthy habits tracker

Month _______________

Year _______________

Days											
31											
32											
33											
34											
35											
36											
37											
38											
39											
40											
41											
42											
43											
44											
45											
46											
47											
48											
49											
50											
51											
52											
53											
54											
55											
56											
57											
58											
59											
60											

Healthy habits tracker

Month ___________

Year ___________

Days											
61											
62											
63											
64											
65											
66											
67											
68											
69											
70											
71											
72											
73											
74											
75											
76											
77											
78											
79											
80											
81											
82											
83											
84											
85											
86											
87											
88											
89											
90											

SOBRIETY ISN'T
AN ANCHOR !
IT'S A PAIR
OF WINGS

I'M
TOO
SOBER
FOR
THIS
SHIT!

Date: _______________   M . T . W . T . F . S . S

One Gole of the day: _______________

How do i feel today? _______________

Today's positive affirmation:

One thing i'm grateful for is:

My mood today : ★ ★ ★ ★ ★   Did i stay sober?   Yes ☐   No ☐

Notes

Date: _____________   M.T.W.T.F.S.S

One Gole of the day: _____________

How do i feel today? _____________

Today's positive affirmation:

One thing i'm grateful for is:

My mood today : ⭐⭐⭐⭐⭐   Did i stay sober?   Yes ☐   No ☐

Notes

Date: ____________________ | M. T. W. T. F. S. S |

One Gole of the day: ____________________

How do i feel today? ____________________

My mood today : ⭐⭐⭐⭐⭐   Did i stay sober?   Yes ☐   No ☐

Notes

Date: _______________   M . T . W . T . F . S . S

One Gole of the day: _______________

How do i feel today? _______________

Today's positive affirmation:

One thing i'm grateful for is:

My mood today : ★ ★ ★ ★ ★   Did i stay sober?   Yes ☐   No ☐

Notes

Date: _______________ [M . T . W . T . F . S . S]

One Gole of the day: _______________

How do i feel today? _______________

Today's positive affirmation:

One thing i'm grateful for is:

My mood today : ⭐⭐⭐⭐⭐   Did i stay sober?   Yes ☐   No ☐

Notes

Date: _______________   M.T.W.T.F.S.S

One Gole of the day: _______________

How do i feel today? _______________

Today's positive affirmation:

One thing i'm grateful for is:

My mood today : ⭐⭐⭐⭐⭐   Did i stay sober?   Yes ☐   No ☐

Notes

Date: ________________   M . T . W . T . F . S . S

One Gole of the day: ________________

How do i feel today? ________________

Today's positive affirmation:

One thing i'm grateful for is:

My mood today : ★★★★★   Did i stay sober?   Yes ☐   No ☐

Notes

Date: _______________   M.T.W.T.F.S.S

One Gole of the day: _______________

How do i feel today? _______________
____
____
____
____
____
____

Today's positive affirmation:

One thing i'm grateful for is:

My mood today : ★★★★★   Did i stay sober?   Yes ☐   No ☐

Notes

Date: _______________   M. T. W. T. F. S. S

One Gole of the day: _______________

How do i feel today? _______________

Today's positive affirmation:

One thing i'm grateful for is:

My mood today : ⭐⭐⭐⭐⭐   Did i stay sober?   Yes ☐   No ☐

Notes

Date: _______________   M . T . W . T . F . S . S

<u>One Gole of the day:</u> _______________

How do i feel today? _______________

Today's positive affirmation:

One thing i'm grateful for is:

My mood today : ⭐⭐⭐⭐⭐   <u>Did i stay sober?</u> Yes ☐ No ☐

Notes

Date: _______________   M . T . W . T . F . S . S

One Gole of the day: _______________

How do i feel today? _______________

Today's positive affirmation:

One thing i'm grateful for is:

My mood today : ⭐⭐⭐⭐⭐   Did i stay sober?   Yes ☐   No ☐

Notes

Date: ___________   M . T . W . T . F . S . S

One Gole of the day: _______________

How do i feel today? _______________

Today's positive affirmation:

One thing i'm grateful for is:

My mood today : ⭐⭐⭐⭐⭐   Did i stay sober?   Yes ☐   No ☐

Notes

Date: ___________ M . T . W . T . F . S . S

One Gole of the day: ___________

How do i feel today?

Today's positive affirmation:

One thing i'm grateful for is:

My mood today : ★ ★ ★ ★ ★   Did i stay sober?   Yes ☐   No ☐

Notes

Date: _______________   M . T . W . T . F . S . S

One Gole of the day: _______________

How do i feel today? _______________

Today's positive affirmation:

One thing i'm grateful for is:

My mood today : ⭐⭐⭐⭐⭐   Did i stay sober?   Yes ☐   No ☐

Notes

Date: _______________   M . T . W . T . F . S . S

One Gole of the day: _______________

How do i feel today? _______________

Today's positive affirmation:

One thing i'm grateful for is:

My mood today : ★ ★ ★ ★ ★   Did i stay sober? Yes ☐ No ☐

Notes

Date: _______________   M.T.W.T.F.S.S

One Gole of the day: _______________

How do i feel today? _______________

My mood today : ★ ★ ★ ★ ★   Did i stay sober?   Yes ☐   No ☐

Today's positive affirmation:

One thing i'm grateful for is:

Notes

Date: _______________

M . T . W . T . F . S . S

One Gole of the day: _______________

How do i feel today? _______________

Today's positive affirmation:

One thing i'm grateful for is:

My mood today : ★★★★★   Did i stay sober?   Yes ☐   No ☐

Notes

Date: _______________   [M . T . W . T . F . S . S]

One Gole of the day: _______________

How do i feel today? _______________

My mood today : ★★★★★   Did i stay sober?   Yes ☐   No ☐

Notes

Date: _______________ | M . T . W . T . F . S . S |

One Gole of the day: _________________________

Today's positive affirmation:

How do i feel today? _________________________

One thing i'm grateful for is:

My mood today : ★ ★ ★ ★ ★   Did i stay sober?   Yes ☐   No ☐

Notes

Date: _______________   M.T.W.T.F.S.S

One Gole of the day: _______________

How do i feel today? _______________

Today's positive affirmation:

One thing i'm grateful for is:

My mood today : ★★★★★   Did i stay sober?   Yes ☐   No ☐

Notes

Date: _______________ M . T . W . T . F . S . S

One Gole of the day: _______________

How do i feel today? _______________

Today's positive affirmation:

One thing i'm grateful for is:

My mood today : ★ ★ ★ ★ ★   Did i stay sober? Yes ☐ No ☐

Notes

Date: ___________ M. T. W. T. F. S. S

One Gole of the day: ___________

How do i feel today? ___________

Today's positive affirmation:

One thing i'm grateful for is:

My mood today : ★★★★★ Did i stay sober? Yes ☐ No ☐

Notes

Date: _______________   M . T . W . T . F . S . S

One Gole of the day: _______________

How do i feel today? _______________

Today's positive affirmation:

One thing i'm grateful for is:

My mood today : ★ ★ ★ ★ ★   Did i stay sober?   Yes ☐   No ☐

Notes

Date: _______________ | M. T. W. T. F. S. S |

One Gole of the day: _______________

How do i feel today? _______________

Today's positive affirmation:

One thing i'm grateful for is:

My mood today : ★★★★★   Did i stay sober?   Yes ☐   No ☐

Notes

Date: _______________   M . T . W . T . F . S . S

One Gole of the day: _______________

How do i feel today? _______________

My mood today : ⭐⭐⭐⭐⭐   Did i stay sober? Yes ☐ No ☐

Today's positive affirmation:

One thing i'm grateful for is:

Notes

Date: _______________   (M . T . W . T . F . S . S)

One Gole of the day: _______________

How do i feel today? _______________

Today's positive affirmation:

One thing i'm grateful for is:

My mood today : ★ ★ ★ ★ ★   Did i stay sober?   Yes ☐   No ☐

Notes

Date: _______________ [M . T . W . T . F . S . S]

One Gole of the day: _________________________

Today's positive affirmation:

How do i feel today? _____________

One thing i'm grateful for is:

My mood today : ⭐⭐⭐⭐⭐   Did i stay sober?   Yes ☐   No ☐

Notes

Date: _______________________   M. T. W. T. F. S. S

One Gole of the day: _______________________

How do i feel today? _______________________

Today's positive affirmation:

One thing i'm grateful for is:

My mood today : ⭐⭐⭐⭐⭐   Did i stay sober?   Yes ☐   No ☐

Notes

Date: _______________   M . T . W . T . F . S . S

One Gole of the day: _______________

How do i feel today? _______________

My mood today : ★ ★ ★ ★ ★   Did i stay sober?   Yes ☐   No ☐

Notes

Date: _______________ [M.T.W.T.F.S.S]

One Gole of the day: _______________

How do i feel today? _______________

My mood today : ⭐⭐⭐⭐⭐   Did i stay sober?   Yes ☐   No ☐

Notes

Date: _______________   M.T.W.T.F.S.S

One Gole of the day: _______________

How do i feel today? _______________

Today's positive affirmation:

One thing i'm grateful for is:

My mood today : ★★★★★   Did i stay sober?   Yes ☐   No ☐

Notes

Date: _______________   M . T . W . T . F . S . S

One Gole of the day: _______________

How do i feel today? _______________

Today's positive affirmation:

One thing i'm grateful for is:

My mood today : ★ ★ ★ ★ ★   Did i stay sober?   Yes ☐   No ☐

Notes

Date: _______

M . T . W . T . F . S . S

One Gole of the day: _______

Today's positive affirmation:

How do i feel today? _______

One thing i'm grateful for is:

My mood today : ⭐⭐⭐⭐⭐   Did i stay sober?   Yes ☐   No ☐

Notes

Date: _______________   M . T . W . T . F . S . S

One Gole of the day: _______________

How do i feel today? _______________

My mood today : ⭐⭐⭐⭐⭐   Did i stay sober? Yes ☐ No ☐

Today's positive affirmation:

One thing i'm grateful for is:

Notes

Date: ___________________   M . T . W . T . F . S . S

One Gole of the day: _______________________

How do i feel today? _______________________

My mood today : ⭐⭐⭐⭐⭐   Did i stay sober?   Yes ☐   No ☐

Notes

Date: ______________   M . T . W . T . F . S . S

One Gole of the day: ______________

How do i feel today? ______________

Today's positive affirmation:

One thing i'm grateful for is:

My mood today : ★ ★ ★ ★ ★   Did i stay sober? ______ Yes ☐ No ☐

Notes

Date: _______________   M . T . W . T . F . S . S

One Gole of the day: _______________

Today's positive affirmation:

How do i feel today? _______________

One thing i'm grateful for is:

My mood today : ★ ★ ★ ★ ★   Did i stay sober?   Yes ☐   No ☐

Notes

Date: _______________   M.T.W.T.F.S.S

One Gole of the day: _______________

How do i feel today? _______________

Today's positive affirmation:

One thing i'm grateful for is:

My mood today : ⭐⭐⭐⭐⭐   Did i stay sober?   Yes ☐   No ☐

Notes

Date: __________

M. T. W. T. F. S. S

One Gole of the day: __________

How do i feel today?

My mood today : ★★★★★   Did i stay sober?   Yes ☐   No ☐

Notes

Date: ___________ M.T.W.T.F.S.S

One Gole of the day: ___________

How do i feel today? ___________

Today's positive affirmation:

One thing i'm grateful for is:

My mood today : ⭐⭐⭐⭐⭐   Did i stay sober?   Yes ☐   No ☐

Notes

Date: _______________   M . T . W . T . F . S . S

One Gole of the day: _______________

How do i feel today? _______________

Today's positive affirmation:

One thing i'm grateful for is:

My mood today : ★★★★★   Did i stay sober? Yes ☐ No ☐

Notes

Date: _______________   M . T . W . T . F . S . S

One Gole of the day: _______________

How do i feel today? _______________

Today's positive affirmation:

One thing i'm grateful for is:

My mood today : ★★★★★   Did i stay sober?   Yes ☐   No ☐

Notes

Date: _______________   M . T . W . T . F . S . S

One Gole of the day: _______________

How do i feel today? _______________

My mood today : ⭐⭐⭐⭐⭐   Did i stay sober?   Yes ☐   No ☐

Notes

Date: _______________   M . T . W . T . F . S . S

One Gole of the day: _______________

How do i feel today? _______________

Today's positive affirmation:

One thing i'm grateful for is:

My mood today : ★ ★ ★ ★ ★   Did i stay sober?   Yes ☐   No ☐

Notes

Date: _______________   M . T . W . T . F . S . S

One Gole of the day: _______________

How do i feel today? _______________

Today's positive affirmation:

One thing i'm grateful for is:

My mood today : ★★★★★   Did i stay sober?   Yes ☐   No ☐

Notes

Date:

M . T . W . T . F . S . S

One Gole of the day:

How do i feel today?

Today's positive affirmation:

One thing i'm grateful for is:

My mood today :   Did i stay sober?   Yes ☐   No ☐

Notes

Date:

M . T . W . T . F . S . S

One Gole of the day:

Today's positive affirmation:

How do i feel today?

One thing i'm grateful for is:

My mood today : ★ ★ ★ ★ ★   Did i stay sober?   Yes ☐   No ☐

Notes

<u>Date:</u> ___________ [M . T . W . T . F . S . S]

<u>One Gole of the day:</u> ___________

How do i feel today?

Today's positive affirmation:

One thing i'm grateful for is:

My mood today : ⭐⭐⭐⭐⭐   Did i stay sober? Yes ☐   No ☐

Notes

Date: _______________   [M . T . W . T . F . S . S]

One Gole of the day: _______________

Today's positive affirmation:
____
____
____
____
____

How do i feel today? _______________
____
____
____
____
____
____

One thing i'm grateful for is:
____
____
____
____
____

My mood today : ★ ★ ★ ★ ★   Did i stay sober?   Yes ☐   No ☐

Notes

____
____
____
____
____
____
____
____
____
____
____
____
____
____
____

Date: _______________ M.T.W.T.F.S.S

One Gole of the day: _______________

How do i feel today? _______________

Today's positive affirmation:

One thing i'm grateful for is:

My mood today : ★★★★★   Did i stay sober?   Yes ☐   No ☐

Notes

Date: _______________   M . T . W . T . F . S . S

One Gole of the day: _______________

How do i feel today? _______________

My mood today : ★★★★★   Did i stay sober?   Yes ☐   No ☐

Notes

Date: _______________   M.T.W.T.F.S.S

One Gole of the day: _______________

Today's positive affirmation:

How do i feel today? _______________

One thing i'm grateful for is:

My mood today : ⭐⭐⭐⭐⭐   Did i stay sober?   Yes ☐   No ☐

Notes

Date: _______________ M . T . W . T . F . S . S

One Gole of the day: _______________

How do i feel today? _______________

Today's positive affirmation:

One thing i'm grateful for is:

My mood today : ★ ★ ★ ★ ★   Did i stay sober?   Yes ☐   No ☐

Notes

Date: _______________ M.T.W.T.F.S.S

One Gole of the day: _______________

How do i feel today? _______________

My mood today : ★★★★★   Did i stay sober? Yes ☐ No ☐

Today's positive affirmation:

One thing i'm grateful for is:

Notes

Date: ____________________   M. T. W. T. F. S. S

One Gole of the day: ____________________

How do i feel today?

____

Today's positive affirmation:

One thing i'm grateful for is:

My mood today : ⭐⭐⭐⭐⭐   Did i stay sober?   Yes ☐   No ☐

Notes

Date: ___________   M . T . W . T . F . S . S

One Gole of the day: _______________

How do i feel today? _______________

Today's positive affirmation:

One thing i'm grateful for is:

My mood today : ★ ★ ★ ★ ★   Did i stay sober?   Yes ☐   No ☐

Notes

Date: _______________   M . T . W . T . F . S . S

One Gole of the day: _____________________

How do i feel today? _______________

Today's positive affirmation:

One thing i'm grateful for is:

My mood today : ⭐⭐⭐⭐⭐   Did i stay sober?   Yes ☐   No ☐

Notes

Date: _______________   (M . T . W . T . F . S . S)

One Gole of the day: _______________

How do i feel today? _______________

My mood today : ⭐⭐⭐⭐⭐   Did i stay sober?   Yes ☐   No ☐

Notes

Date: _______________   M. T. W. T. F. S. S

One Gole of the day: _______________

How do i feel today? _______________

Today's positive affirmation:

One thing i'm grateful for is:

My mood today : ★ ★ ★ ★ ★   Did i stay sober?   Yes ☐   No ☐

Notes

Date: ___________   M.T.W.T.F.S.S

One Gole of the day: ___________

How do i feel today? ___________

My mood today : ⭐⭐⭐⭐⭐   Did i stay sober?   Yes ☐   No ☐

Notes

Date: _______________ [M . T . W . T . F . S . S]

One Gole of the day: _________________

How do i feel today? ___________________

Today's positive affirmation:

One thing i'm grateful for is:

My mood today : ★ ★ ★ ★ ★   Did i stay sober?   Yes ☐   No ☐

Notes

Date: ___________ M.T.W.T.F.S.S

One Gole of the day: _______________

How do i feel today? _______________

My mood today : ★★★★★   Did i stay sober? Yes ☐ No ☐

Today's positive affirmation:

One thing i'm grateful for is:

Notes

Date:

M. T. W. T. F. S. S

One Gole of the day:

Today's positive affirmation:

How do i feel today?

One thing i'm grateful for is:

My mood today : Did i stay sober? Yes ☐ No ☐

Notes

Date: _______________ $\boxed{M.T.W.T.F.S.S}$

<u>One Gole of the day:</u> _______________

How do i feel today? _______________

<u>Today's positive affirmation:</u>

<u>One thing i'm grateful for is:</u>

My mood today : ★ ★ ★ ★ ★   <u>Did i stay sober?</u>   Yes ☐   No ☐

Notes

Date: _______________   M. T. W. T. F. S. S

One Gole of the day: _________________________

<table>
<tr><td>

How do i feel today? ___________________

</td><td>

Today's positive affirmation:

One thing i'm grateful for is:

</td></tr>
</table>

My mood today : ★ ★ ★ ★ ★   Did i stay sober?   Yes ☐   No ☐

Notes

Date: _______________   M . T . W . T . F . S . S

One Gole of the day: _______________

How do i feel today? _______________

Today's positive affirmation:

One thing i'm grateful for is:

My mood today : ⭐⭐⭐⭐⭐   Did i stay sober?   Yes ☐   No ☐

Notes

Date: _______________   M. T. W. T. F. S. S

One Gole of the day: _______________

How do i feel today?

My mood today : ★★★★★   Did i stay sober?   Yes ☐   No ☐

Notes

Date: ___________   M.T.W.T.F.S.S

One Gole of the day: _______________

Today's positive affirmation:

How do i feel today? _______________

One thing i'm grateful for is:

My mood today : ⭐⭐⭐⭐⭐   Did i stay sober?   Yes ☐   No ☐

Notes

Date: _______________   M . T . W . T . F . S . S

One Gole of the day: _______________

How do i feel today? _______________

Today's positive affirmation:

One thing i'm grateful for is:

My mood today : ⭐⭐⭐⭐⭐   Did i stay sober? Yes ☐ No ☐

Notes

<u>Date:</u> __________   M . T . W . T . F . S . S

<u>One Gole of the day:</u> __________

How do i feel today? __________

Today's positive affirmation:

One thing i'm grateful for is:

My mood today : ★ ★ ★ ★ ★   Did i stay sober?   Yes ☐   No ☐

Notes

Date:

M . T . W . T . F . S . S

One Gole of the day:

Today's positive affirmation:

How do i feel today?

One thing i'm grateful for is:

My mood today :   ★★★★★   Did i stay sober?   Yes ☐   No ☐

Notes

Date: _______________   M.T.W.T.F.S.S

One Gole of the day: _______________

How do i feel today? _______________

My mood today : ⭐⭐⭐⭐⭐   Did i stay sober?   Yes ☐   No ☐

Today's positive affirmation:

One thing i'm grateful for is:

Notes

Date: _______________   M . T . W . T . F . S . S

One Gole of the day: _______________

How do i feel today? _______________

Today's positive affirmation:

One thing i'm grateful for is:

My mood today : ⭐⭐⭐⭐⭐   Did i stay sober?   Yes ☐   No ☐

Notes

Date: _______________   M. T. W. T. F. S. S

One Gole of the day: _______________

How do i feel today?

My mood today : ★★★★★   Did i stay sober?   Yes ☐   No ☐

Today's positive affirmation:

One thing i'm grateful for is:

Notes

Date: _____________   M . T . W . T . F . S . S

One Gole of the day: _____________

Today's positive affirmation:

How do i feel today? _____________

One thing i'm grateful for is:

My mood today : ⭐⭐⭐⭐⭐   Did i stay sober?   Yes ☐   No ☐

Notes

Date: _______________ M.T.W.T.F.S.S

One Gole of the day: _______________

How do i feel today? _______________

Today's positive affirmation:

One thing i'm grateful for is:

My mood today : ★★★★★   Did i stay sober?   Yes ☐   No ☐

Notes

Date:

M. T. W. T. F. S. S

One Gole of the day:

Today's positive affirmation:

How do i feel today?

One thing i'm grateful for is:

My mood today : Did i stay sober? Yes ☐ No ☐

Notes

Date:

M.T.W.T.F.S.S

One Gole of the day:

Today's positive affirmation:

How do i feel today?

One thing i'm grateful for is:

My mood today :

Did i stay sober?   Yes ☐   No ☐

Notes

Date: __________________   [M . T . W . T . F . S . S]

One Gole of the day: __________________

How do i feel today?

Today's positive affirmation:

One thing i'm grateful for is:

My mood today : ⭐⭐⭐⭐⭐   Did i stay sober?   Yes ☐   No ☐

Notes

Date: _______________   M . T . W . T . F . S . S

One Gole of the day: _______________

How do i feel today? _______________

Today's positive affirmation:

One thing i'm grateful for is:

My mood today : ★ ★ ★ ★ ★   Did i stay sober?   Yes ☐   No ☐

Notes

Date: _______________ M . T . W . T . F . S . S

One Gole of the day: _______________

How do i feel today? _______________

Today's positive affirmation:

One thing i'm grateful for is:

My mood today : ★ ★ ★ ★ ★   Did i stay sober?   Yes ☐   No ☐

Notes

Date: _______________   M . T . W . T . F . S . S

Today's positive affirmation:

One Gole of the day: _______________

How do i feel today? _______________

One thing i'm grateful for is:

My mood today : ⭐⭐⭐⭐⭐   Did i stay sober?   Yes ☐   No ☐

Notes

Date: _______________   M . T . W . T . F . S . S

One Gole of the day: _______________

How do i feel today? _______________

My mood today : ★ ★ ★ ★ ★   Did i stay sober?   Yes ☐   No ☐

Notes

<u>Date:</u> _______________   [M . T . W . T . F . S . S]

<u>One Gole of the day:</u> _______________________________

How do i feel today? _______________________________
____
____
____
____
____
____
____
____

Today's positive affirmation:
____
____
____
____
____
____

One thing i'm grateful for is:
____
____
____
____
____

My mood today : ★ ★ ★ ★ ★   Did i stay sober?   Yes ☐   No ☐

Notes

____
____
____
____
____
____
____
____
____
____
____
____
____
____
____

Date: _______________   M . T . W . T . F . S . S

One Gole of the day: _________________

Today's positive affirmation:

How do i feel today? _________________

One thing i'm grateful for is:

My mood today : ★★★★★   Did i stay sober?   Yes ☐   No ☐

Notes

Date: _______________   M . T . W . T . F . S . S

One Gole of the day: _______________

How do i feel today? _______________

My mood today : ⭐⭐⭐⭐⭐   Did i stay sober?   Yes ☐   No ☐

Notes

Date: _______________   [M. T. W. T. F. S. S]

One Gole of the day: _______________

How do i feel today? _______________

____
____
____
____
____
____

Today's positive affirmation:
____
____
____
____

One thing i'm grateful for is:
____
____
____
____

My mood today : ★ ★ ★ ★ ★   Did i stay sober? Yes ☐ No ☐

Notes

____
____
____
____
____
____
____
____
____
____
____
____
____
____
____
____
____

Date: ____________ M. T. W. T. F. S. S

One Gole of the day: ____________

How do i feel today? ____________

Today's positive affirmation:

One thing i'm grateful for is:

My mood today : ★★★★★   Did i stay sober? Yes ☐ No ☐

Notes

Date: _______________ M . T . W . T . F . S . S

One Gole of the day: _______________

How do i feel today? _______________

Today's positive affirmation:

One thing i'm grateful for is:

My mood today : ★ ★ ★ ★ ★   Did i stay sober?   Yes ☐   No ☐

Notes

Date: ___________ | M . T . W . T . F . S . S |

One Gole of the day: ________________________

Today's positive affirmation:

How do i feel today? ________________

One thing i'm grateful for is:

My mood today : ★ ★ ★ ★ ★   Did i stay sober?   Yes ☐   No ☐

Notes

Date: ______________ M . T . W . T . F . S . S

One Gole of the day: ____________________

How do i feel today? ____________________

Today's positive affirmation:

One thing i'm grateful for is:

My mood today : ⭐⭐⭐⭐⭐   Did i stay sober?   Yes ☐   No ☐

Notes

Date: _______________   M . T . W . T . F . S . S

One Gole of the day: _______________

How do i feel today? _______________

My mood today : ★ ★ ★ ★ ★   Did i stay sober?   Yes ☐   No ☐

Today's positive affirmation:

One thing i'm grateful for is:

Notes

Date: _______________   M . T . W . T . F . S . S

One Gole of the day: _______________

How do i feel today? _______________

Today's positive affirmation:

One thing i'm grateful for is:

My mood today : ⭐⭐⭐⭐⭐   Did i stay sober?   Yes ☐   No ☐

Notes

Date: _______________   M. T. W. T. F. S. S

<u>One Gole of the day:</u> _______________

How do i feel today? _______________

My mood today : ⭐⭐⭐⭐⭐   Did i stay sober?   Yes ☐   No ☐

Notes

One day at a Time

I
CAN
DO
IT

FUCK
ADDICTION

GOOD
VIBES
ONLY

I'M
ADDICTED
TO
BETTERING
MY SELF

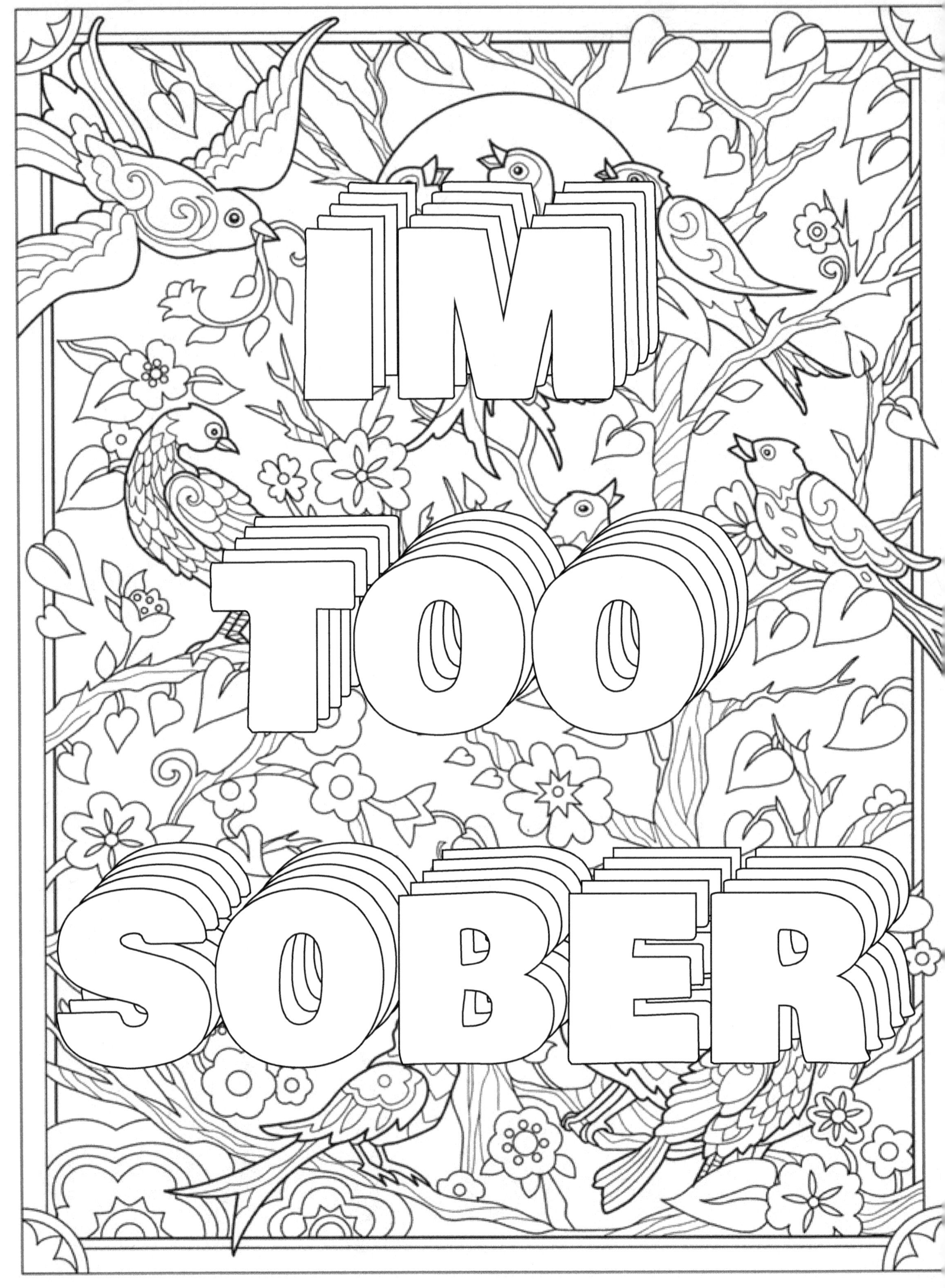

I'M
TOO
SOBER

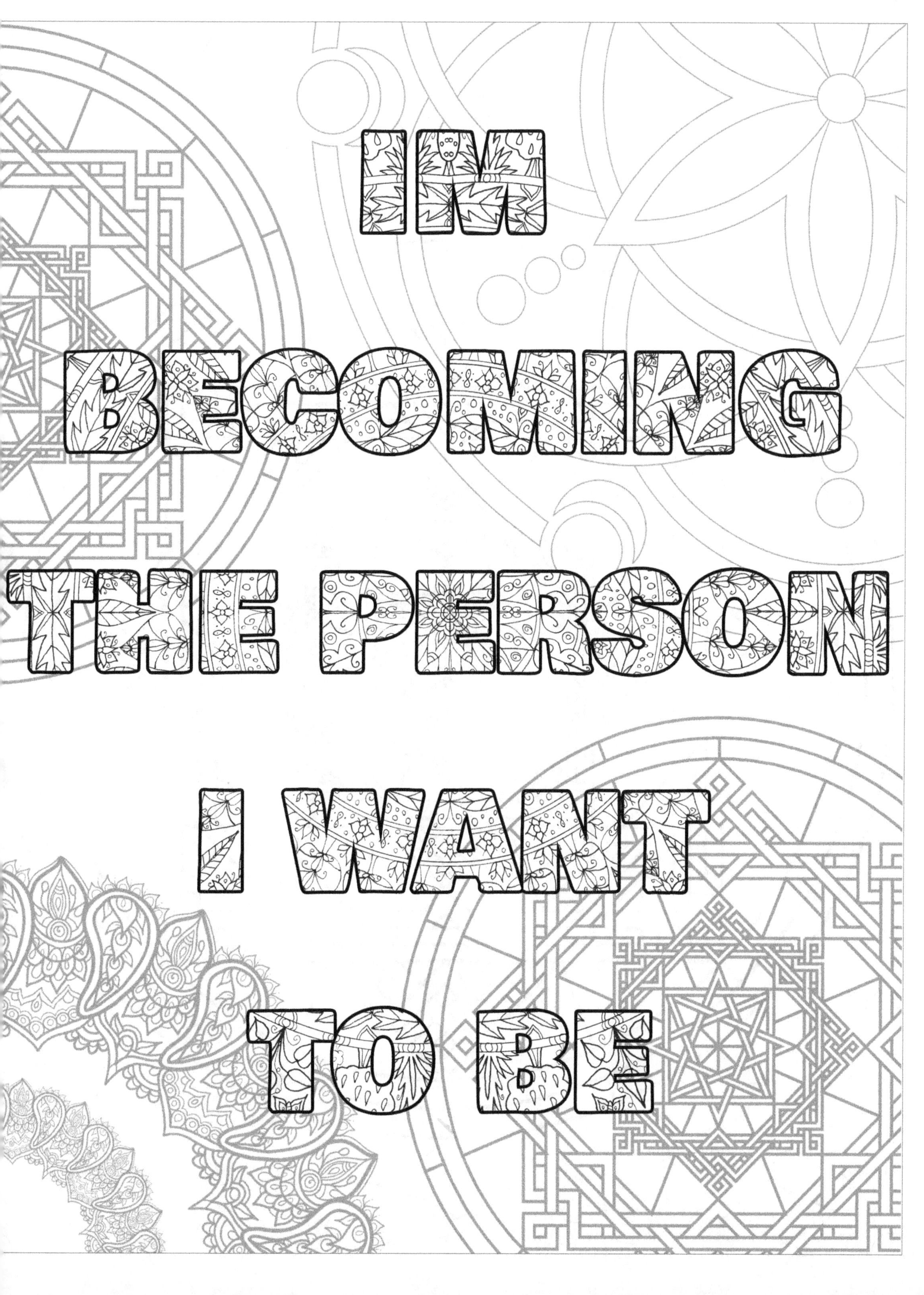
IM BECOMING THE PERSON I WANT TO BE

TODAY
IT HURTS
TOMORROW
IT WORKS

I CAN DO THIS AND I WILL DO THIS

CONTROL
THE
NARRATIVE
OF MY
LIFE

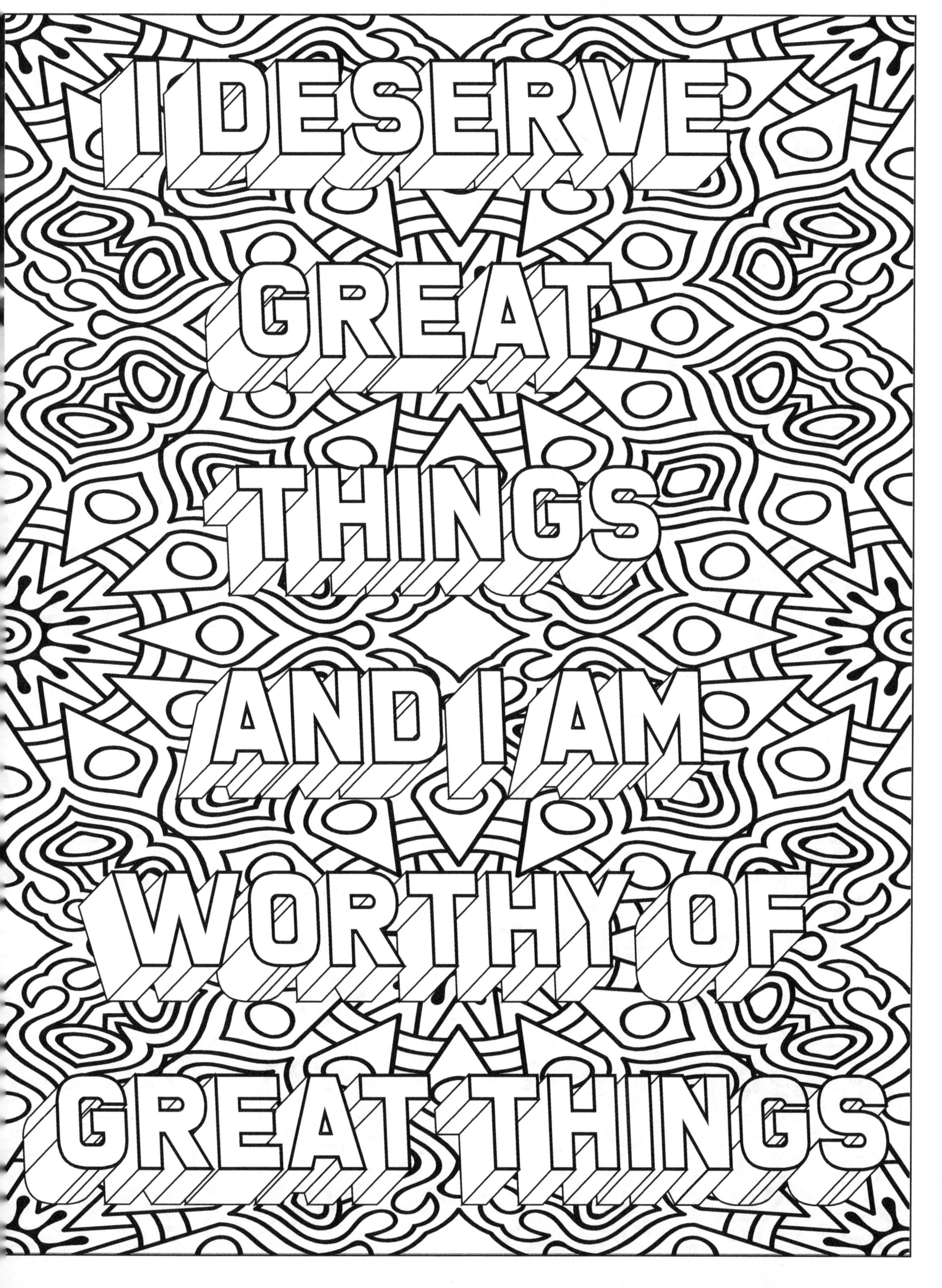

I DESERVE
GREAT
THINGS
AND I AM
WORTHY OF
GREAT THINGS

I AM
STRONG

I'M STRONG
I'M STRONG

START
THINKING
WELLNES
NOT ILLNESS

SOBRIETY ISN'T
AN ANCHOR !
IT'S A PAIR
OF WINGS

I'M
TOO
SOBER
FOR
THIS
SHIT !

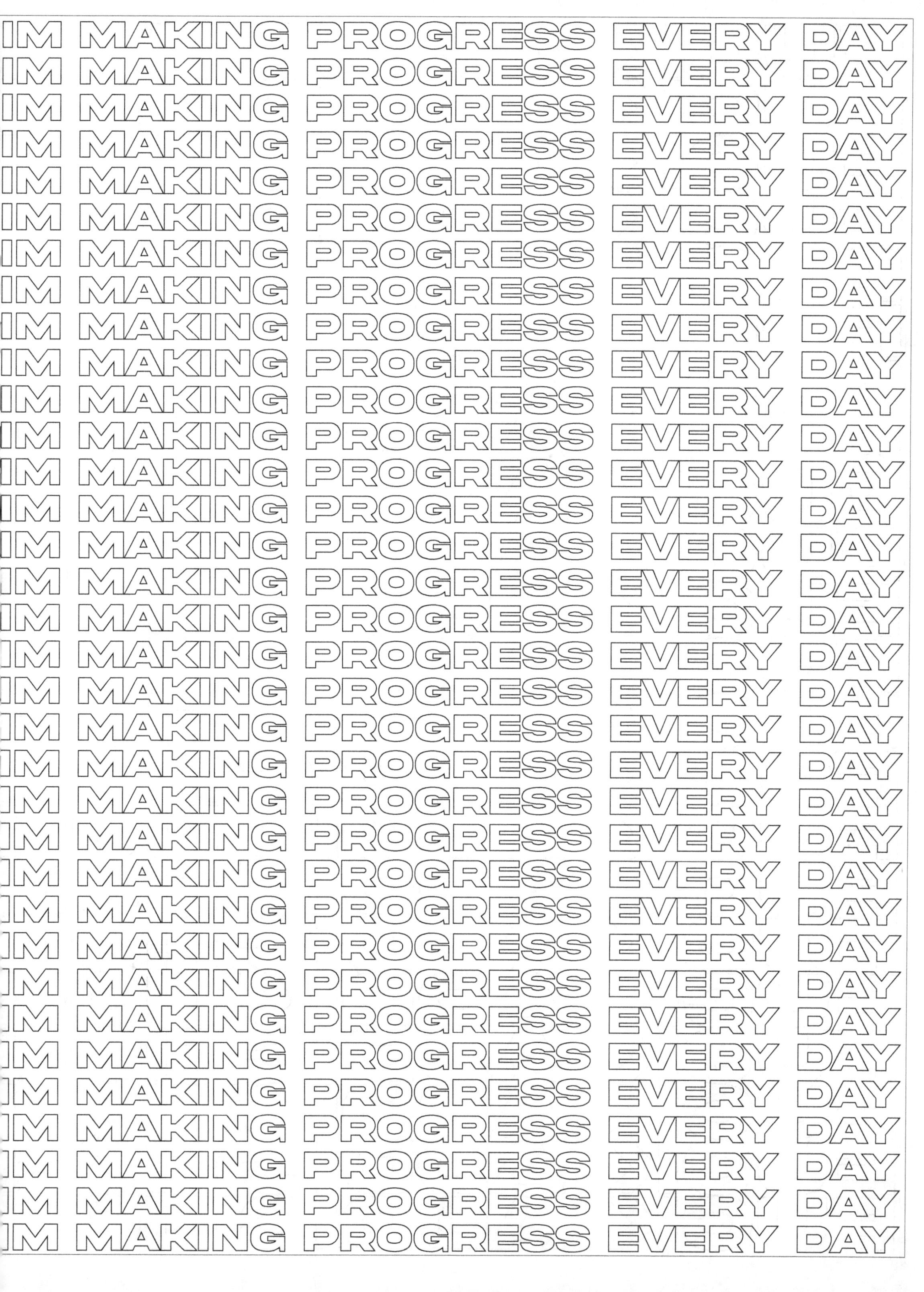

IM MAKING PROGRESS EVERY DAY
IM MAKING PROGRESS EVERY DAY
IM MAKING PROGRESS EVERY DAY
IM MAKING PROGRESS EVERY DAY
IM MAKING PROGRESS EVERY DAY
IM MAKING PROGRESS EVERY DAY
IM MAKING PROGRESS EVERY DAY
IM MAKING PROGRESS EVERY DAY
IM MAKING PROGRESS EVERY DAY
IM MAKING PROGRESS EVERY DAY
IM MAKING PROGRESS EVERY DAY
IM MAKING PROGRESS EVERY DAY
IM MAKING PROGRESS EVERY DAY
IM MAKING PROGRESS EVERY DAY
IM MAKING PROGRESS EVERY DAY
IM MAKING PROGRESS EVERY DAY
IM MAKING PROGRESS EVERY DAY
IM MAKING PROGRESS EVERY DAY
IM MAKING PROGRESS EVERY DAY
IM MAKING PROGRESS EVERY DAY
IM MAKING PROGRESS EVERY DAY
IM MAKING PROGRESS EVERY DAY
IM MAKING PROGRESS EVERY DAY
IM MAKING PROGRESS EVERY DAY
IM MAKING PROGRESS EVERY DAY
IM MAKING PROGRESS EVERY DAY
IM MAKING PROGRESS EVERY DAY
IM MAKING PROGRESS EVERY DAY
IM MAKING PROGRESS EVERY DAY
IM MAKING PROGRESS EVERY DAY
IM MAKING PROGRESS EVERY DAY
IM MAKING PROGRESS EVERY DAY
IM MAKING PROGRESS EVERY DAY
IM MAKING PROGRESS EVERY DAY
IM MAKING PROGRESS EVERY DAY
IM MAKING PROGRESS EVERY DAY
IM MAKING PROGRESS EVERY DAY
IM MAKING PROGRESS EVERY DAY
IM MAKING PROGRESS EVERY DAY
IM MAKING PROGRESS EVERY DAY

FUCK ADDICTION
FUCK ADDICTION
FUCK ADDICTION
FUCK ADDICTION
FUCK ADDICTION
FUCK ADDICTION
FUCK ADDICTION
FUCK ADDICTION
FUCK ADDICTION
FUCK ADDICTION
FUCK ADDICTION
FUCK ADDICTION
FUCK ADDICTION
FUCK ADDICTION
FUCK ADDICTION
FUCK ADDICTION
FUCK ADDICTION
FUCK ADDICTION
FUCK ADDICTION
FUCK ADDICTION
FUCK ADDICTION
FUCK ADDICTION
FUCK ADDICTION

Printed in the USA
CPSIA information can be obtained
at www.ICGtesting.com
CBHW061937121223
2596CB00011B/116